Abusive Leadership

SpiritBuilt Leadership 6

Malcolm Webber

Published by:

Strategic Press
www.StrategicPress.org

Strategic Press is a division of Strategic Global Assistance, Inc.
www.sgai.org

513 S. Main St. Suite 2
Elkhart, IN 46516
U.S.A.

+1-844-532-3371 (LEADER-1)

Copyright © 2002 Malcolm Webber

ISBN 978-1-888810-45-5

All Scripture references are from the New International Version of the Bible, unless otherwise noted.

+1-844-532-3371 (LEADER-1)

Table of Contents

Introduction 7

1. "Not So With You!" 9
2. Leadership and Power 13
3. Security in Christ and Leadership 15
4. The Role of Insecure Followers 21
5. The Power of the Supernatural 25
6. The Downward Spiral of Exploitation 27
7. The Stark Contrast 29
8. The Heart of the Matter 41
9. Some Questions to Ask Yourself 47
10. To Avoid Being an Abusive Leader 53

Introduction

In Matthew 20:25-28, Jesus said that leadership in the Kingdom of God is of a fundamentally different *nature* than the leadership of the world. Unfortunately, the leadership that is present in so many churches is not only "worldly" in its authoritarianism; it is often *worse* than worldly leadership and downright abusive.

The purpose of this book is to expose abusive leadership in the church. Our approach is not the usual anecdotal one taken in books with a similar purpose; we have tried to build conceptual frameworks that reveal the very *heart* of what constitutes both abusive and servant leadership.

This is the sixth of a series of books on leadership. Together, they comprise the series, *SpiritBuilt Leadership*.

Our prayer is that this series of books will be effective in assisting Christian men and women around the world to be the mighty leaders God has called them to be.

Malcolm Webber, Ph.D.
Strategic Press
Elkhart, Indiana
February, 2002

chapter 1

"Not So With You!"

Kingdom leadership stands in contrast to worldly leadership patterns, in so far as they involve "lording it over" others:

> *Jesus called them together and said, "You know that the rulers of the Gentiles lord it over them, and their high officials exercise authority over them. Not so with you. Instead, whoever wants to become great among you must be your servant..." (Matt. 20:25-26; cf. Is. 55:8-9; 30:1-2; 31:1)*

A godly leader is firm and strong but he does not dominate the people of God. However, a leader who is insecure in his relationship with God and with others may compensate by domination and dictatorship over God's people. There are clear New Testament warnings against tyrannizing, overbearing, bullying, controlling or possessing the people of God.

In Revelation, Jesus spoke against the Nicolaitans:

> *But you have this in your favor: You hate the practices of the Nicolaitans, which I also hate. (Rev. 2:6)*

> *Nevertheless, I have a few things against you: You have people there who hold to the teaching of Balaam, who taught Balak to entice the Israelites to sin by eating food sacrificed to idols and by committing sexual immorality. Likewise you also have those who hold to the teaching of the Nicolaitans. (Rev. 2:14-15)*

The word "nicolaitan" means "conquest, victory or triumph over the people." These people appeared to have established dominating leadership over God's people.

Another New Testament example of abusive leadership was Diotrephes, whose pride and self-exaltation resulted in a public spirit of exclusivism and unteachableness:

> *I wrote to the church, but Diotrephes, who loves to be first, will have nothing to do with us. So if I come, I will call attention to what he is doing, gossiping maliciously about us. Not satisfied with that, he refuses to welcome the brothers. He also stops those who want to do so and puts them out of the church. Dear friend, do not imitate what is evil but what is good. Anyone who does what is good is from God. Anyone who does what is evil has not seen God. (3 John 9-11)*

A close study of these three verses yields the following characteristics of an abusive leader:

- He loves to be first and seeks the pre-eminence (cf. Matt. 23:5-12).
- He refuses to submit to godly authority.
- He gossips and slanders others, especially those who are perceived as rival authorities. He is threatened by them.
- He fears outside input and teachings.
- He controls the actions of those in his group.
- He expels those who will not submit to his control.

In Ezekiel 34:1-16, God condemns the leaders who didn't care for the people but exploited them for their own personal benefit.

> *…Woe to the shepherds of Israel who only take care of themselves! Should not shepherds take care of the flock? You eat the curds, clothe yourselves with the wool and slaughter the choice animals, but you do not take care of the flock. You have not strengthened the weak or healed the sick or bound up the injured. You have not brought back the strays or searched for the lost. You have ruled them harshly and brutally. So they were scattered because there was no shepherd, and when they were scattered they became food for all the wild animals. (Ezek. 34:2-5)*

> ...my shepherds did not search for my flock but cared for themselves rather than for my flock, (Ezek. 34:8)

In Zephaniah 3:3, God condemns the leaders who "are evening wolves, who leave nothing for the morning." In other words, they devour the people completely so that nothing is left; unlike wolves that would usually leave some bones to gnaw on. These leaders totally plundered the people.

> *Her officials are roaring lions, her rulers are evening wolves, who leave nothing for the morning. (Zeph. 3:3)*

Similar condemnations of leaders are found in other Old Testament Scriptures:

> *...Listen, you leaders of Jacob, you rulers of the house of Israel. Should you not know justice, you who hate good and love evil; who tear the skin from my people and the flesh from their bones; who eat my people's flesh, strip off their skin and break their bones in pieces; who chop them up like meat for the pan, like flesh for the pot? (Mic. 3:1-3)*

> *There is a conspiracy of her princes within her like a roaring lion tearing its prey; they devour people, take treasures and precious things and make many widows within her. (Ezek. 22:25)*

> *Her officials within her are like wolves tearing their prey; they shed blood and kill people to make unjust gain. (Ezek. 22:27)*

There are also New Testament warnings against this kind of leadership:

> *The hired hand is not the shepherd who owns the sheep. So when he sees the wolf coming, he abandons the sheep and runs away. Then the wolf attacks the flock and scatters it. The man runs away because he is a hired hand and cares nothing for the sheep. (John 10:12-13)*

To the elders among you, I appeal as a fellow elder, a witness of Christ's sufferings and one who also will share in the glory to be revealed: Be shepherds of God's flock that is under your care, serving as overseers – not because you must, but because you are willing, as God wants you to be; not greedy for money, but eager to serve; not lording it over those entrusted to you, but being examples to the flock. And when the Chief Shepherd appears, you will receive the crown of glory that will never fade away. (1 Pet. 5:1-4)

The former preach Christ out of selfish ambition, not sincerely... (Phil. 1:17)

I call God as my witness that it was in order to spare you that I did not return to Corinth. Not that we lord it over your faith, but we work with you for your joy, because it is by faith you stand firm. (2 Cor. 1:23-24)

In fact, you even put up with anyone who enslaves you or exploits you or takes advantage of you or pushes himself forward or slaps you in the face. (2 Cor. 11:20)

I know that after I leave, savage wolves will come in among you and will not spare the flock. Even from your own number men will arise and distort the truth in order to draw away disciples after them. So be on your guard!... (Acts 20:29-31)

... shepherds who feed only themselves... (Jude 12)

These men are grumblers and faultfinders; they follow their own evil desires; they boast about themselves and flatter others for their own advantage.(Jude 16)

chapter 2

Leadership and Power

An abusive leader is one who tends to centralize authority and derive power from position, control of rewards and coercion. In contrast, a servant leader gives authority away to others, encourages participation in decision making, relies on others' knowledge and initiation for completion of tasks, and depends on love and respect for influence.

Leaders have a choice: they can hold onto their power and use it purely for selfish ends, or they can give their power away to others. Paradoxically, leaders become more powerful when they give their own power away. They don't lose anything – in fact, everyone benefits!

Leadership power is not a fixed and limited sum (like a pie that can be cut into only so many pieces) to be hoarded and grudgingly divided up only when absolutely necessary. A leader's power is not reduced when he empowers others. Organizationally, power actually expands and multiplies when it is shared with others. When people have responsibility and genuine influence, their commitment to the organization and its success drastically increases. The key to unleashing an organization's potential to excel is putting the power in the hands of the people who perform the work. Thus, leaders must trust and respect their constituents, and they must know their people well enough to empower them appropriately. Jesus is our ultimate Model for this; He did not wait until His disciples were perfect before He gave them authority (Matt. 10:1; 28:18-20; Mark 16:15-20; etc.). Thus, servant leaders who take the power that flows to them and connect it to others, become power generators from which their constituents draw strength.

People who have authoritarian leaders will not feel empowered, but distrusted and used. Consequently, they will tend to do what is expected of them only as long as the leader is personally present to supervise them. Moreover, they will usually be discontented with the close, autocratic style of leadership and feelings of hostility will arise. However, people who have servant leaders tend to do what is expected of them even when the leader is absent – since the people have been genuinely empowered with personal responsibility and authority, resulting in a high level of personal ownership – and they will have more positive feelings towards their leader.

chapter 3

Security in Christ and Leadership

The most central and important characteristic of a healthy leader is a strong personal relationship with Jesus Christ.[1] Servant leaders lead out of a deep and abiding security in Christ. Abusive leaders, however, usually are very insecure. There are other reasons why certain leaders become abusive, but insecurity is one of the main ones – especially in the church.

Spiritual leadership must be the natural *expression* of the divine calling. It must not be for the purpose of *proving* to everyone else – or even to the leader himself – that the leader possesses the calling.

How can you tell which you are?

- When someone rejects your leadership, how do you feel? Personally rejected? Does it hurt your feelings that you personally are not received by someone as a leader? Do you personally identify with your ministry?
- What does it mean to you to be a leader, or to have a ministry? Why are you seeking a ministry? Does it mean that you "count" now, that you are "important" now? Or that now you simply have a positive responsibility to fulfill? Which one? What does your response indicate?
- When you encounter conflict in your leadership, does it feel like a competitive game and test of wills with others or a healthy dialogue and positive debate? What does your answer tell you about yourself and your leadership?

---

[1] This truth is examined in *Healthy Leaders: SpiritBuilt Leadership #2*.

- If you often take questions as challenges, does that reveal an underlying insecurity?

In true leadership, the *purpose* is the central issue. In abusive leadership, the *person* of the leader becomes the central issue.

How can you tell which you are?

- When a task that you say represents your vision is successfully accomplished by someone else, are you as happy about it as when it is accomplished by you? For example, are you as pleased about the church down the road leading many people to the Lord, as you are when your own church does this? Does your answer indicate whether your vision is purely purpose-based or person- (self-) based?

   And I saw that all labor and all achievement spring from man's envy of his neighbor. This too is meaningless, a chasing after the wind. (Eccl. 4:4)

The servant leader truly serves his people by leading them in such a way that their best interests are served and they find fulfillment. The essence of abusive leadership, however, is that the leader uses the followers for his own selfish purposes.

   Even as I please all men in all things, not seeking mine own profit, but the profit of many, that they may be saved. (1 Cor. 10:33)

   ...the Son of Man did not come to be served, but to serve, and to give his life as a ransom for many. (Mark 10:45)

The servant leader will articulate a vision that serves the interests of the whole organization. Seeing himself as fundamentally equal with his followers, he will lead in a non-self-aggrandizing manner, and he will actively empower and develop his people. The abusive leader, on the other hand, is domineering and narcissistic. He has high needs for power, driven in part by his own personal lack of peace and security in Christ, and will promote goals that reflect his own self-interests. He will play on his followers' needs as a means to achieve his own interests (Acts 20:30). He will largely disregard the feelings of others, and will demand unquestioning obedience and dependence in his followers.

How can you tell which you are?

- Who will really benefit as a result of your leadership or ministry or a specific decision? Yourself or the people? In what specific ways?
- Are you actually empowering people? Or does everyone need your permission to do everything? Do you give them permission to do it their own way or only your way?

The abusive leader will frequently emphasize identification with, and devotion to, *himself* over a more straightforward embracing of the values and goals he is ostensibly promoting.

> *For we do not preach ourselves, but Jesus Christ as Lord, and ourselves as your servants for Jesus' sake. (2 Cor. 4:5)*

How can you tell which you are?

- Who do you talk about? Who do you promote? Yourself, others, the Lord Jesus? What can you learn from this?

Regarding vision, problems occur when domineering leaders possess an exaggerated sense of the opportunities for their vision, when they grossly underestimate the resources necessary for its accomplishment, or when they seriously underestimate the obstacles that stand in the way of its fulfillment. In addition, visions often fail when they reflect largely the leader's needs rather than the legitimate needs and aspirations of his constituents. A self-absorbed leader may also be unable to recognize fundamental shifts occurring within or around his organization that demand redirection of the vision.

Abusive leaders are prone to exaggerated self-descriptions and claims for their visions, which can mislead their followers. For example, they may present information that makes their visions appear more feasible or appealing than they are in reality. They may screen out looming problems or foster an illusion of control when things actually are out of control. In these ways abusive leaders manipulate, and ultimately take advantage of, their followers.

Organizations led by such leaders, inevitably fail to achieve these lofty visions. Frequently this results in the people becoming bitter and disillusioned and vowing to never commit themselves to a leader again: "I was used once, but never again!"

Some abusive leaders cause dysfunctional rivalries by promoting antagonistic "in" and "out" groups within their organization – usually the distinction is the issue of extreme "loyalty" to themselves personally.[2] One hallmark of the abusive leader is absolutist polarizing rhetoric, drawing his followers together against the perceived "enemy."

Other abusive leaders create excessive dependence on themselves and then alternate between idealizing and devaluing dependent subordinates – particularly those who report directly to them.

How can you tell which you are?

- Do you promote rivalries based on loyalty to you? Perhaps you don't promote them but do you stop such rivalries if they begin?

Domineering leaders often have a difficult time developing successors. They simply enjoy "center stage" too much to share it. Sometimes they will have a "puppet" understudy, but to find a replacement who is a genuine peer may be too threatening for such narcissistic leaders.

---

[2] This sometimes happens within a family with husband and wife vying for the loyalty of the children.

The root and fruit of both healthy and abusive leadership are summarized in the following table:

The Root and Fruit of Abusive Leadership		
	The Healthy Leader	**The Abusive Leader**
The Root:	Security in Christ	Personal insecurity
The Fruit:		
Leadership is…	The simple *expression* of God's calling	To *prove* God's calling
Central issue is…	The *purpose* of the leader	The *person* of the leader
Leader's vision…	Serves God & the organization	Serves the leader
Leader sees himself as…	Equal to followers	Above followers
Leader promotes…	Identification with values and goals	Identification with himself
Leader creates…	Internal inclusiveness	"In" and "out" groups
Power is…	Given away to others	Centralized in leader
Follower capacities are…	Independent of leader	Dependent on leader
Leadership succession is…	In place	Undeveloped

chapter 4

The Role of Insecure Followers

In the face of abusive leadership, followers may react in one of three ways:

1. They may perceive the abusiveness and refuse to comply with it. Some may resist openly either through direct confrontation or through "whistle blowing" to a higher authority. Others may quietly leave the organization, not wishing to be part of a "fight."

2. They may perceive the leader's actions as abusive but comply with him despite their perceptions. Thus, they will obey the leader and outwardly endorse his views and actions, while secretly disagreeing. They may be too afraid of the leader (or those "with" the leader) or too uncertain of themselves to make an open move of disagreement. They may also have some vested personal interest in going along with the abusiveness.[3] Perhaps all their friends are in the organization. In certain cultures, people allow their leaders to exhibit large amounts of obvious abusiveness and still follow them. One man, when asked why he was continuing to follow a leader who he acknowledged had serious problems, replied, "In our culture, the leader is the father; we're the children. Children follow their father."

3. They may both outwardly and inwardly accept the behaviors, views and demands of the leader. They believe the leader's

---

[3] Like the lackeys in the story of *The Emperor's New Clothes*.

actions are reasonable, even when those actions are blatantly self-serving and undermine others. Their occasional skepticism is easily swept away by the leader's persuasive arguments and rationalizations. Such followers have had their belief systems infiltrated by the leader who is thus enabled to get away with increasingly extreme ideas, actions and demands.

Abusive leaders would not exist if no one followed them! Without followers, an abusive leader would be nothing but an empty shell, "full of sound and fury, signifying nothing."

Insecure followers who look to their leaders as "parent" figures, seeking their approval and acceptance, are what make abusive leadership possible. Their insecurity causes their vulnerability. They are not secure in Christ, so they look to the leader for their identity and security. Such followers are willing to give their leaders inordinate amounts of control over their personal lives and relationships, and over their belief systems. Often they will suspend their own individual judgments and follow unquestioningly the dictates of the leader. Sometimes they will even begin to adopt the personal characteristics of their leader.[4] Certainly, it is appropriate to imitate the characteristics of a good leader related to his character, values, lifestyle, dedication to God, and so forth (1 Cor. 11:1; 2 Thess. 3:7-9; Heb. 13:7), but it is dysfunctional to imitate his personal quirks![5]

Insecure followers are willing to give the extreme personal "loyalty" their leaders demand and constantly feel guilty that they may be weakening in their loyalty. They willingly take the blame for any failure of the leader's vision and scold themselves every time the leader questions their loyalty: "If you were really committed, you would...!"

---

[4] It should be noted that healthy leaders can also have unhealthy or immature followers who possess some of these characteristics. When the leader perceives this unhealthy relationship that others may have with him, he must do all he can to confront and transform it into a godly relationship.
[5] The followers of one abusive leader went so far as to imitate his choice of running shoes and his favorite brand of peanut butter!

Not having found a sense of secure acceptance in Christ, these followers are highly motivated to seek the leader's personal approval and are highly affected by the leader's actions, beliefs and even mood swings. Their personal vulnerability to their leader goes far beyond what would be considered normal in the leader-follower relationship. This extreme vulnerability enhances the leader's ability to alter and abuse the follower's perceptions, emotions and thoughts.

Thus, follower-insecurity creates the *opportunity* for abusiveness that leader-insecurity *takes advantage of.* The solution, in both cases, is repentance and security in Christ. Healthy leader-follower relationships must be based upon a mutual recognition and experience of the centrality and all-sufficiency of the Person of Jesus Christ.

To the Victims

People who have been the victims of abusiveness in churches, denominations, marriages, families or jobs, should consider two things:

1. The leader hurt the follower out of his own insecurity. He was probably not intentionally trying to hurt the person.

2. A large part of the problem lay in the follower and his own insecurity. Insecure people cannot hurt those who are secure in Christ.

Consequently, the solution for a person who is still "hurting" from having been abused in this way in the past is to forgive the abuser and then to let God set him free from insecurity, finding deep security in Christ, so it will not happen again.[6]

---

[6] Unfortunately, it is not uncommon for an insecure individual who has been disappointed by the discovery of defects in an idolized leader, to cast him aside and search for a new hero, to whom he attaches himself in the hope that he will not be disappointed again. The only solution to this cycle is to find security in Christ.

chapter 5

The Power of the Supernatural

Churches are quite prone to the rise of abusive leadership – particularly churches that embrace the supernatural. This is because the presence of the supernatural in the life of a leader – in the form of healings, deliverances, the prophetic, etc. – can confirm his higher symbolic status in the eyes of his followers, and open the way for a considerably more dysfunctional leader-follower relationship. There can be a strong sense that to reject the leader is to reject God, and therefore to invite His sternest judgment. This strengthens the fear and compliance of followers. Abusive leaders in a supernatural context are prone to using such threats as, "Don't touch God's anointed!" This helps them to avoid any questions or accountability. After all, who would argue with God?

The sense of the grandiose "power" of the leader is especially appealing to insecure followers who want someone else to rescue them and take care of them. Moreover, the leader represents what the follower wants to be. Thus, his success becomes the follower's success, protecting the follower from confronting his own inadequate relationship with God.

Because churches are filled with people who (rightly so) acknowledge their weaknesses and need for help, Christian leaders who are gifted in supernatural ways by God must particularly guard against the rise of abusive tendencies in their hearts.

chapter 6

The Downward Spiral of Exploitation

Domineering leaders often entangle their followers in a downward spiral of exploitation. First, they offer a grandiose vision and confidently encourage followers to accomplish it. Followers, however, soon find themselves in an untenable position. Because of their leader's optimism, they have underestimated the constraints facing the mission as well as the resources they need but currently lack. As a result, performance inevitably falls short of the leader's high expectations. Wishing to comply with their leader's wishes, however, followers continue to strive. Soon, their performance appears substandard as they fall behind.

Although initially the leader will blame the outside world or the devil for undermining the mission, his attention will eventually turn to the followers. Conditioned to accept their leader's viewpoint and not to challenge it, followers willingly receive the blame from their leader. Over time, they begin to "learn helplessness." Believing themselves inherently deficient, they lose hope for future endeavors and lose confidence in their own ability to successfully obey God and fulfill His will. Thus, instead of building up and empowering his followers, the leader gradually destroys them and creates highly (and helplessly) dependent individuals.

This downward spiral is depicted in the following graphic.

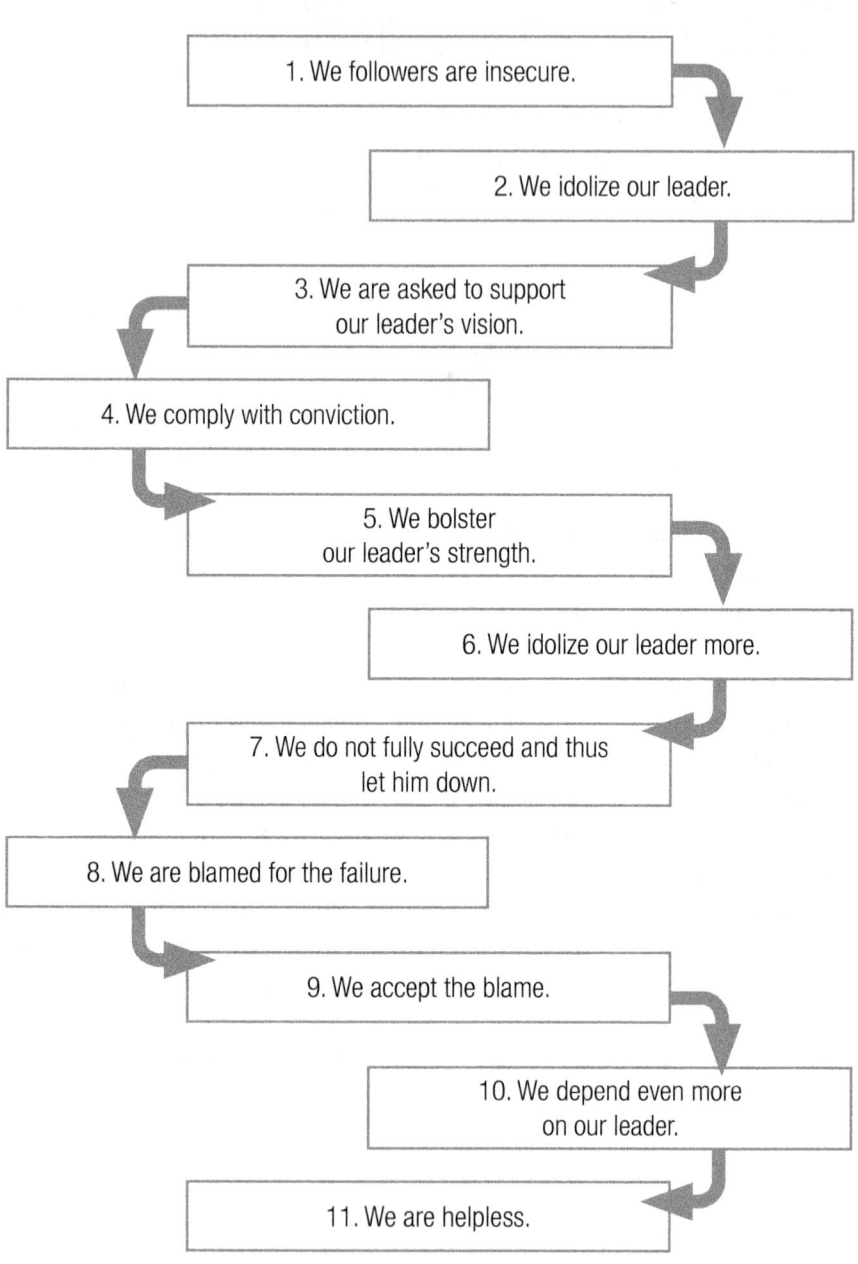

chapter 7

The Stark Contrast

According to our original definition, there are three parts to leadership[7]:

1. The leader establishes the direction.

2. He aligns the people in that direction.

3. He motivates and inspires them to move in that direction and to fulfill the vision.

Servant leaders differ from abusive leaders in all three basic issues of leadership: direction, alignment and achievement. They also have significant personal differences. Finally, there are profound differences in the impact of each kind of leader on the followers.[8]

Direction

The servant leader leads, ultimately, for the benefit of others, in the fulfillment of God's will. Thus, he is a "servant" leader. The abusive leader, however, leads, ultimately, for his own benefit. Servant leaders pursue visions that benefit their organizations, whereas abusive leaders build their own power base at the expense of the organization.

---

[7] These three aspects of leadership were explained in *Leadership: SpiritBuilt Leadership #1*.
[8] One does not need to possess *all* the characteristics that follow to be a truly abusive leader. The presence of *any* of these characteristics in his life or leadership should concern a leader.

In developing their vision, servant leaders are responsive to the interests and desires of their followers. They incorporate their followers' hopes, dreams and aspirations in their vision. Followers actively contribute to and develop the vision further so that it becomes truly shared by all.

Abusive leaders derive their visions solely from within themselves. Their goals promote their own personal agenda often to the disadvantage of others. In the extreme, the leader's vision is pursued without question and no matter what damage is caused to others. Any effort he makes at seeking consensus is only a superficial and symbolic "going through the motions."

Servant leaders desire to invest in others to see the vision accomplished. Jesus' hope was for His followers to do "greater things" than He had accomplished (John 14:12). Moreover, the time frame of His vision was future; it was only after His ascension that His followers "turned the world upside down" (Acts 17:6). Thus, He was not merely doing things for *His own* accomplishment *now* – He built others for *their* accomplishments in the *future*.

Abusive leaders, however, want to see results now. They need the affirmation and significance they think the results will bring. Their vision is more short term and revolves around numbers and outward success.

The servant leader is willing to live and die in obscurity, investing a few, focusing on them and not on himself, knowing that if he does this properly the fruit will come eventually, perhaps after he is gone (Matt. 13:31-32). He is willing to lead for the long term. He is willing to lead for the few.

The abusive leader demands impressive results now. Impacting a few is not enough for him. He leads for the short term. He leads only for the many.

Direction	
Servant Leader	**Abusive Leader**
Leads, ultimately, for the benefit of others.	Leads, ultimately, for his own benefit.
His vision serves the interests of the whole organization.	His vision reflects his own self-interest.
Promotes realistic visions.	Promotes visions that are often grandiose and unrealistic.
Works with coworkers toward long-range goals, with concern for their personal development.	Demands immediate results, even if it damages the coworker's future potential.
Focuses on a few.	Focuses on many.
Leads changes very carefully and cautiously for the sake of followers.	Arbitrarily changes at the whim of his own need or desire.
Encourages loyalty to Jesus Christ.	Mouths the need for loyalty to Christ; in reality, demands personal loyalty to himself.

Alignment

The issue of alignment involves helping the people to understand and embrace the direction.

In setting agendas that represent the interests of the organization, servant leaders continuously seek out the viewpoints of their followers on critical issues. They want to have the right vision and they want everyone to own it. Thus, they listen to the ideas, needs, aspirations and wishes of followers and then, within the context of their own secure and well-developed system of beliefs, respond in an appropriate way. They invite two-way communication with others, while still promoting a sense of knowing what they are doing. In this way, servant leaders build a broad understanding and ownership of the vision and a strong commitment to it. People do not follow such leaders because they are ordered to do so, or because they calculate that such compliance is in their own self-interest, but they voluntarily identify with the organization and its vision, and willingly seek to fulfill its purpose.

In contrast, abusive leaders unilaterally establish the vision and then impose it on everyone, demanding compliance.

Alignment	
Servant Leader	**Abusive Leader**
Emphasizes internalization of the vision by changing coworkers' core attitudes, beliefs and values.	Emphasizes compliance of behavior and identification with himself.
Concentrates on influence from *within* by encouraging, inspiring and motivating.	Depends on external controls from *without*, using restrictions and rules.
Desires power *with* coworkers.	Desires power *over* coworkers.
Elicits genuine and inward ownership of the vision.	Often elicits public compliance without private conviction.

Achievement

The issue of the achievement of the vision involves helping the people begin to move and then keeping them moving in the right direction, so that the organization's purposes are fulfilled.

Servant leaders see the potential in their followers who they perceive as coworkers and treat with respect. They are sensitive and responsive to their followers' needs and aspirations and share both information and opportunities with them. In this way, they achieve higher levels of ability, motivation and commitment.

Abusive leaders, however, are not so concerned with their followers. Self-focused, they are insensitive and unresponsive to the needs, hopes and desires of others. Often they are arrogant and harsh.

> *Do not rebuke an older man harshly, but exhort him as if he were your father. Treat younger men as brothers, older women as mothers, and younger women as sisters, with absolute purity. (1 Tim. 5:1-2)*

In 1 Timothy 5, Paul shows that a healthy leader values the relationship between believers far above any need to assert or prove his own authority. The leader must not use the depersonalizing "tongue-lashing," which method of correction relies on fear and authority and is often used when feelings of anger and insecurity are involved.

Servant leaders express confidence in followers' abilities to achieve the vision, and when it is met, they recognize the contributions of others and share the credit for success.

Abusive leaders have a low opinion of others and take all the credit for any organizational successes that are achieved.

Achievement	
Servant Leader	**Abusive Leader**
Has a good relationship with coworkers, showing respect for the individual.	Relates to coworkers from an "I'm superior – you're inferior" attitude.
Wisely and selflessly uses organizational resources for the benefit of all.	Manipulates organizational resources for personal gain. Denies followers their share of opportunities and rewards.
Values individual workers, encourages and praises them, rather than condemns them for every mistake.	Has a low opinion of coworkers and is very critical of others' mistakes.
Facilitates through empowerment.	Controls through unilateral decisions.

Achievement	
Servant Leader	**Abusive Leader**
Celebrates learning.	Points to errors.
Lifts and supports.	Pushes and drives.
Listens.	Lectures.
Dialogues with people.	Talks at people.
Stimulates creativity using purpose to inspire commitment.	Triggers insecurity using fear to achieve compliance.
Encourages input and feedback.	Wants no constructive criticism, seeing it as a challenge.
Gives coworkers credit for the results.	Takes credit for all accomplishments.
Promotes respect and honor toward those who have left the organization even if there were significant problems.[9]	Openly attacks and makes examples of those who have "betrayed" him or left the organization in "disloyalty." Will use verses like 1 John 2:19 when referring to his betrayers and detractors.
Empowers others for the organization's and their own benefit.	Avoids work by "dumping" tasks and responsibilities on others.
Desires organizational effectiveness but not at the expense of the people.	Pushes people to burnout while reaping the rewards of their efforts.

Personal Qualities

Servant leaders are secure in Christ. Consequently, their focus is not themselves but others. Abusive leaders, however, are insecure. Because of their insecurity, their agendas revolve around themselves. They are characterized by self-absorption, self-protection and self-interest.

Because they are secure in Christ, servant leaders exercise power in

---

[9] For example, one of the marks of a healthy church is that you can leave it without being branded as a "traitor" and without feeling that you're going to lose your salvation or at least your part in God's purposes.

constructive ways to serve others. They are more concerned about genuinely contributing to the welfare of their followers than they are about promoting their own dominance, status or prestige.

In contrast, abusive leaders exercise power in dominant and authoritarian ways to serve their own interests, to manipulate others for their own purposes and to win at all costs. Although they know how to mouth the right religious slogans related to servanthood, in reality they are preoccupied with "looking out for number one." They use power for personal gain and exercise it in a dominant and controlling manner. The life of the organization revolves around them – not their visions but their persons.

The two kinds of leaders also differ in their moral standards, which influence their decisions. Servant leaders follow biblical principles of truth, which may go against the majority opinion. Such leaders are not swayed by popular opinion unless it is in line with biblical principles. They are internally consistent, acting in concert with their values and beliefs. Moreover, they promote a vision that inspires followers to accomplish collective objectives that will help the organization and promote Kingdom agendas. Their vision is driven by "doing what is right" as opposed to "doing the right thing" for the moment. Through their example of high moral standards, they develop the moral principles, standards and conduct of their followers.

Abusive leaders, however, follow standards if they satisfy their immediate self-interests. They are skilled at managing an impression that what they are doing conforms to what others consider "the right thing to do." They are often excellent communicators and are able to manipulate others to support their personal agendas.

Servant leaders are realistic in appraising their own abilities and limitations. They learn from criticism rather than being fearful of it, welcoming both positive and negative feedback. They are open to advice, seek accountability, and are willing to have their initial judgments challenged. Leaders who are secure in Christ have the confidence to encourage contrary opinions and can enhance themselves through the strengths of others.

Abusive leaders, however, have an inflated sense of their own importance, thrive on attention and admiration from others and shun contrary opinions. They attract and gravitate towards followers who are loyal, affectionate and uncritical. They seek to create loyal supporters and eliminate all dissenters. They are unwilling to have their strategies questioned and expect and even demand that their decisions be accepted without question. Moreover, they will avoid genuine accountability, feeling personally threatened by it.

To succeed in such an organization, followers soon learn to offer the leader only the information he wants to hear, whether or not it is correct. In extreme cases, even critical information may be withheld because of the leader's intolerance and intimidation, resulting in organizational disaster.

When an abusive leader succeeds in some organizational endeavor, he is often further confirmed in his central abusive tendencies by the accolades that accompany his accomplishments. If he believes the praises heaped on him, he will be further seduced by delusions of greatness. Each time the admiring crowd shouts its approval of him, the leader's façade of invincibility is strengthened. There is a mutually-reassuring intoxication as the followers are mesmerized by the leader's success and the leader is mesmerized by the enraptured adoration of his followers. Rather than focusing on the next challenge, he becomes preoccupied with maintaining an aura of greatness. Image management replaces active, meaningful leadership of the organization.

Servant leaders, however, are secure in Christ and so do not need the praises of men. Instead, they deliberately avoid the trappings of success, choosing to stay little in their own eyes. Moreover, their followers who have been strengthened in their capacities for responsible thought and initiative, provide critical input to their leader – balancing encouragement with reality (in contrast to the flattery that the abusive leader surrounds himself with) – which may keep him from straying down the wrong path.

Personal Qualities	
Servant Leader	**Abusive Leader**
Secure in Christ.	Personally insecure.
Is considerate and concerned for others.	Is concerned primarily with himself.
Studies the stress that others are under to help alleviate it if possible.	Constantly elicits sympathy for himself over his own stress and hardships.
Willing to discuss his decisions and the reasons for them, unless circumstances do not allow.	Interprets questions as personal criticism or disloyalty.
Tries to work with the initially uncooperative, seeing their positive potential.	Quickly discards individuals who he perceives will not embrace his vision or conform to his agenda.
Trusting toward people; thinks the best.	Suspicious toward people, sometimes to the point of paranoia.
Vulnerability is power.	Knowledge is power.
Communicates freely and openly.	Withholds or conceals information when it does not suit his purposes.
Responds to problems with prayer and investigation.	Responds to problems with anger and accusation.
Responds to failure by taking personal responsibility.	Responds to failure by blaming others.
Knows he must earn the support of his followers.	Demands unchallenged support.
Welcomes appropriate accountability.	Threatened by any attempts at real accountability.

The Effect of Leaders: Developing or Enslaving Others?

Servant leaders genuinely desire to empower and develop their followers. Their ultimate goal is to convert followers into leaders.

The goal of the servant leader is to bring the best potential out of people. Often they will see more potential in people than those people see in themselves. They provide opportunities for them to develop, and personally help them to grow in their creative and critical thinking abilities. They encourage their followers to view the world from different perspectives which, as leader, they themselves may not have previously considered. They ask them to challenge the status quo and to question the traditional ways of solving problems by reevaluating the assumptions they use to understand and analyze a problem.

By expressing confidence in their followers' abilities to accomplish organizational goals, and by encouraging them to think on their own and to question the established ways of doing things, they create people who can think independently and lead others effectively. With a servant leader, people feel confident and capable. They eventually take responsibility for their own decisions and actions, taking bolder initiatives and exploring new paths. Following the leader's example, they establish their own set of internal standards, in line with the Scriptures, that guide their beliefs and behaviors. Finally, they begin to develop others around them as leaders.

The goal of abusive leaders, however, is to have obedient, dependent and compliant followers. They undermine followers' motivation and ability to challenge existing views, to engage in their own development and growth, and to develop independent perspectives. Ultimately, the followers' sense of personal identity and worth becomes inextricably connected to supporting the achievement of the leader's vision. If the leader deviates into unethical conduct in achieving his vision, followers are unlikely to question his actions. Since the leader is the moral standard-bearer, followers can rationalize even the most destructive of actions.

The impact of leaders on followers is often more extreme during crises. Followers of a servant leader enter crises with a greater willingness to analyze the problem and offer solutions to the leader. Since they have been encouraged all along to take responsibility, during a crisis they are more confident and able to offer counsel to the leader. They provide the needed checks and balances concerning the leader's decisions. Since people trust servant leaders, they will rally behind the leader's decisions when there is no time to deliberate during crisis. In addition, crises are not used by servant leaders to blame followers for their inadequacies. Rather, they use crises to develop strength and a sense of purpose in their overall vision. Crises often reveal the leader's fundamental intention to do what is right. Once the crisis has passed, servant leaders use it as a learning experience. They point to the need for followers to develop their own capabilities so that future crises can be avoided, dealt with more effectively, or handled by followers themselves when the leader is unavailable.

For the abusive leader, a crisis situation is often ripe for gaining or solidifying his power base. This power base can then be used politically to secure the leader's personal agenda and to minimize dissent among followers. Insecure followers easily become dependent on the leader who provides a clear action plan during crisis. After the crisis subsides, followers increasingly rely on the leader for direction. They lose any confidence they once had to question the leader's thinking and decisions. Thus, their dependence on the leader is increased even more.

Their Effect	
Servant Leader	**Abusive Leader**
Encourages coworkers to depend on God for themselves.	Creates an atmosphere where the coworkers are permanently dependent on him, thus giving him a sense of power and importance.
Promotes emotional independence from himself.	Promotes emotional dependence on himself. Consequently, others are intimidated by his moodiness.
Liberates the individual, encourages ideas and participation.	Limits individual freedoms, prefers to make all the decisions.
Equips people to be fruitful.	Does not train others to function effectively and independently.
Builds an organization characterized by joy and creativity.	Builds an organization characterized by fear and conformity.

chapter 8

The Heart of the Matter

Abusive leaders are not called so because they beat the people or yell at them or call them names. Servant leaders are not called so because they serve their followers breakfast in bed every morning.[10]

The essence of abusiveness in leadership is using followers for the leader's own interests.

> *...Woe to the shepherds of Israel who only take care of themselves! Should not shepherds take care of the flock? You eat the curds, clothe yourselves with the wool and slaughter the choice animals, but you do not take care of the flock. You have not strengthened the weak or healed the sick or bound up the injured. You have not brought back the strays or searched for the lost. You have ruled them harshly and brutally. So they were scattered because there was no shepherd...my flock lacks a shepherd and so has been plundered and has become food for all the wild animals, and because my shepherds did not search for my flock but cared for themselves rather than for my flock, (Ezek. 34:2-8)*
>
> *See how each of the princes of Israel who are in you uses his power to shed blood. (Ezek. 22:6)*

---

[10] In spite of popular misconceptions, "servant leadership" does not mean that the leader "sweeps the floor" all the time. This distinction is clear from Jesus' life and ministry: Jesus slept in the boat while the others rowed (Matt. 8:23-24), He broke the bread and the disciples distributed it to the multitudes (Matt. 14:19), He sent Peter fishing for the tax money (Matt. 17:27) and the disciples prepared for the Passover (Matt. 26:17-19). In addition, when Jesus washed His disciples' feet in John 13, it was clearly an exceptional, unprecedented event (John 13:7-8).

*This is what the L*ORD *says: "As for the prophets who lead my people astray, if one feeds them, they proclaim 'peace'; if he does not, they prepare to wage war against him." (Mic. 3:5)*

Her leaders judge for a bribe, her priests teach for a price, and her prophets tell fortunes for money. (Mic. 3:11)

The hired hand is not the shepherd who owns the sheep. So when he sees the wolf coming, he abandons the sheep and runs away. Then the wolf attacks the flock and scatters it. The man runs away because he is a hired hand and cares nothing for the sheep. (John 10:12-13)

I know that after I leave, savage wolves will come in among you and will not spare the flock. Even from your own number men will arise and distort the truth in order to draw away disciples after them. So be on your guard!... (Acts 20:29-31)

For such people are not serving our Lord Christ, but their own appetites. By smooth talk and flattery they deceive the minds of naive people. (Rom. 16:18)

In fact, you even put up with anyone who enslaves you or exploits you or takes advantage of you or pushes himself forward or slaps you in the face. (2 Cor. 11:20)

The former preach Christ out of selfish ambition, not sincerely... (Phil. 1:17)

I have no one else like him [i.e. Timothy], who takes a genuine interest in your welfare. For everyone looks out for his own interests, not those of Jesus Christ. (Phil. 2:20-21)

In their greed these teachers will exploit you with stories they have made up... (2 Pet. 2:3)

The essence of servant leadership is seeking what is best for the followers in the purposes of God, and not oneself.

> *...the Son of Man did not come to be served, but to serve, and to give his life as a ransom for many. (Mark 10:45)*
>
> *Even as I please all men in all things, not seeking mine own profit, but the profit of many, that they may be saved. (1 Cor. 10:33)*
>
> *I call God as my witness that it was in order to spare you that I did not return to Corinth. Not that we lord it over your faith, but we work with you for your joy, because it is by faith you stand firm. (2 Cor. 1:23-24)*
>
> *For we do not preach ourselves, but Jesus Christ as Lord, and ourselves as your servants for Jesus' sake. (2 Cor. 4:5)*
>
> *All this is for your benefit, so that the grace that is reaching more and more people may cause thanksgiving to overflow to the glory of God. (2 Cor. 4:15)*
>
> *...what I want is not your possessions but you. After all, children should not have to save up for their parents, but parents for their children. So I will very gladly spend for you everything I have and expend myself as well... (2 Cor. 12:14-15)*
>
> *Did I exploit you through any of the men I sent you? I urged Titus to go to you and I sent our brother with him. Titus did not exploit you, did he? Did we not act in the same spirit and follow the same course? (2 Cor. 12:17-18)*
>
> *...everything we do, dear friends, is for your strengthening. (2 Cor. 12:19)*
>
> *It is right for me to feel this way about all of you, since I have you in my heart; for whether I am in chains or defending and confirming*

> *the gospel, all of you share in God's grace with me. God can testify how I long for all of you with the affection of Christ Jesus. (Phil. 1:7-8)*

> *...I know that I will remain, and I will continue with all of you for your progress and joy in the faith, so that through my being with you again your joy in Christ Jesus will overflow on account of me. (Phil. 1:25-26)*

> *But even if I am being poured out like a drink offering on the sacrifice and service coming from your faith, I am glad and rejoice with all of you. (Phil. 2:17)*

> *For now we really live, since you are standing firm in the Lord. (1 Thess. 3:8)*

> *To the elders among you, I appeal as a fellow elder, a witness of Christ's sufferings and one who also will share in the glory to be revealed: Be shepherds of God's flock that is under your care, serving as overseers – not because you must, but because you are willing, as God wants you to be; not greedy for money, but eager to serve; not lording it over those entrusted to you, but being examples to the flock. And when the Chief Shepherd appears, you will receive the crown of glory that will never fade away. (1 Pet. 5:1-4)*

Thus, an abusive leader may actually be quite nice toward the people, but be using them for his own agenda. For example, a pastor of a small church who is only using that church as a stepping-stone to "greater things," is, by definition, an abusive leader. He is only using the people to serve his own interests. He has no long-term commitment to what is best for the people he leads.

The servant leader, however, serves God by serving others.

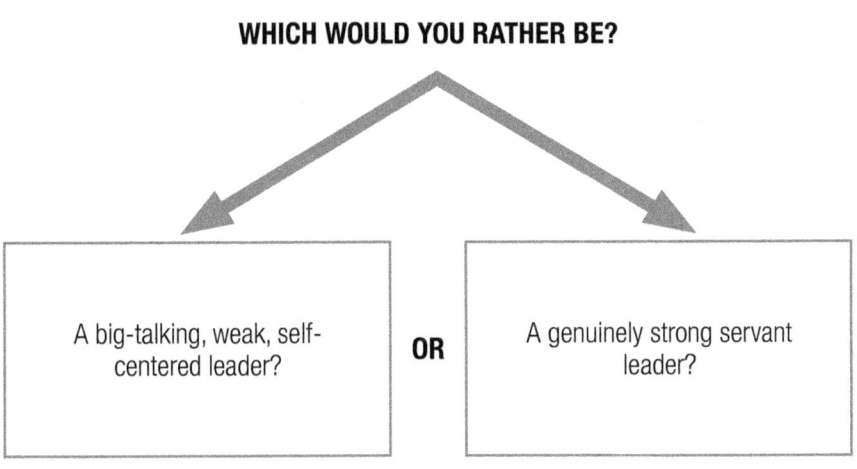

chapter 9

Some Questions to Ask Yourself

1. Which kind of leader – abusive or servant – are you?

   _____

2. Why do you say that?

   _____

   _____

   _____

   _____

3. Who will really benefit as a result of your leadership? Yourself or your followers? In what specific ways?

   _____

   _____

   _____

   _____

4. When you encounter conflict in your leadership, does it feel like a competitive game and test of wills with others or a healthy dialogue and positive debate? What does your answer tell you about yourself and your leadership?

_____

_____

_____

_____

5. When someone rejects your leadership, how do you feel? Personally rejected? What does that indicate?

_____

_____

_____

_____

6. What does it mean to you to be a leader? Does it mean that you "count" now? Or that now you simply have a positive responsibility to fulfill? Which one? What does your response indicate?

_____

_____

_____

_____

7. Is your leadership purely the *expression* of your calling in God, or is there any element of *proving* in your heart?

_____

_____

_____

_____

8. Is it more fulfilling for you to do the actual work of the ministry (winning the lost, planting churches, etc.) or to tell others about what you have done?

_____

_____

_____

_____

9. Is your leadership birthed entirely from security in Christ or are there elements of insecurity in your heart?

_____

_____

_____

_____

10. Who is the focus of any public speaking that you do? Yourself, others, the Lord Jesus? What can you learn from this?

11. Are you actually empowering people? Or does everyone need your permission to do everything? Do you give them permission to do it their own way or only your way?

12. When a task that you say represents your vision is successfully accomplished by someone else, are you as happy about it as when it is accomplished by you (Phil. 1:14-18)? For example, are you as pleased about the church down the road leading many people to the Lord, as you are when your own church does this? Does your answer indicate whether your vision is purely purpose-based or person- (self-) based?

13. No one is perfect, so we can assume that all of us have exhibited a mixture of some aspects of both kinds of leadership at some point. What elements of abusiveness have you exhibited in the past?

_____

_____

_____

_____

14. What were the results?

_____

_____

_____

_____

15. Are there *any* elements of abusiveness in your present leadership? Please go over the lists of characteristics again as you consider this question.

_____

_____

_____

_____

16. Who could you ask to determine this for sure? When will you ask them about this?

_____

_____

_____

_____

chapter 10

To Avoid Being an Abusive Leader

It should be noted that most Christian leaders – as imperfect people – will probably exhibit aspects of abusive leadership at some point. Therefore, the godly leader, knowing that he is not above this tendency, should consciously and deliberately take the following steps to avoid being abusive at all:

1. Prayer. It is hard to know our own hearts and motives. We must remain continually in prayer, asking God to expose what is really happening inside our lives and ministries.

   Pray that I may be rescued from the unbelievers in Judea and that my service in Jerusalem may be acceptable to the saints there, (Rom. 15:31)

2. Study the example of the Lord Jesus Christ. He is the perfect Model of true leadership at all points.

   I am the good shepherd. The good shepherd lays down his life for the sheep. (John 10:11)

3. Humility. The great antidote for abusive leadership is 1 Corinthians 3:7.

   So neither he who plants nor he who waters is anything, but only God, who makes things grow.

4. Commitment. The godly leader must be committed to God, to his followers, and to inward reality in his own life. Especially during decision-making, he must remain unfailingly committed to truth, not allowing himself to be influenced by expediency, convenience or selfishness. The Holy Spirit will help us do this (Rom. 8:13).

> ... if by the Spirit you put to death the misdeeds of the body, you will live, (Rom. 8:13)
>
> And we, who with unveiled faces all reflect the Lord's glory, are being transformed into his likeness with ever-increasing glory, which comes from the Lord, who is the Spirit. (2 Cor. 3:18)

5. Awareness. The Christian leader must develop the ability to distinguish between personal issues and an organizationally-based vision in his beliefs and actions. He must be acutely aware of his own vested interests at all times and strive to crucify them if they are not consistent with the interests of the people he says he is serving.

> My conscience is clear, but that does not make me innocent. It is the Lord who judges me. Therefore judge nothing before the appointed time; wait till the Lord comes. He will bring to light what is hidden in darkness and will expose the motives of men's hearts. At that time each will receive his praise from God. (1 Cor. 4:4-5)

6. Responsibility. The healthy leader will spend significant time and effort in assisting his followers' development *separate from* his personal mission. In truth, the Christian mission is people-development.[11]

---

[11] Ultimately to the glory of God and the fulfillment of His will, of course.

> *It was he who gave some to be apostles, some to be prophets, some to be evangelists, and some to be pastors and teachers, to prepare God's people for works of service, so that the body of Christ may be built up until we all reach unity in the faith and in the knowledge of the Son of God and become mature, attaining to the whole measure of the fullness of Christ. (Eph. 4:11-13)*

7. Self-evaluation. The leader should accurately and honestly assess his own contributions to both successful and unsuccessful outcomes – rather than merely blaming others. Even good leaders may tend to avoid looking at their own contribution to poor performance. Moreover, the godly leader should address follower discomfort and poor performance that are often signals for his own need of self-reevaluation – particularly in the area of communication.

   > *Wherefore we labour, that, whether present or absent, we may be accepted of him. For we must all appear before the judgment seat of Christ; that every one may receive the things done in his body, according to that he hath done, whether it be good or bad. Knowing therefore the terror of the Lord, we persuade men; but we are made manifest unto God; and I trust also are made manifest in your consciences. (2 Cor. 5:9-11)*

8. Continual prayer, reflection and heart breaking before the Lord. God will keep us honest and pure. The leader must conscientiously seek to catch himself any time he is tempted to take advantage of his role and power.

   > *So I strive always to keep my conscience clear before God and man. (Acts 24:16)*

   > *…We are sure that we have a clear conscience and desire to live honorably in every way. (Heb. 13:18)*

9. Genuine accountability. Abusive leaders will often happily submit to those who they know share their views. In contrast, servant leaders will seek out balanced and honest counselors who are not afraid to disagree and to hold them genuinely accountable.

> *Fourteen years later I went up again to Jerusalem, this time with Barnabas. I took Titus along also. I went in response to a revelation and set before them the gospel that I preach among the Gentiles. But I did this privately to those who seemed to be leaders, for fear that I was running or had run my race in vain. (Gal. 2:1-2)*

Exercises

1. What changes do you need to make in your life and ministry?

   _____

   _____

   _____

   _____

   _____

   _____

   _____

2. What specific commitments can you make that will help you bring these changes to pass?

   _____

   _____

   _____

   _____

   _____

   _____

   _____

Books in the *SpiritBuilt Leadership* Series
by Malcolm Webber, Ph.D.

1. ***Leadership.*** Deals with the nature of leadership, servant leadership, and other basic leadership issues.

2. ***Healthy Leaders.*** Presents a simple but effective model of what constitutes a healthy Christian leader.

3. ***Leading.*** A study of the practices of exemplary leaders.

4. ***Building Leaders.*** Leaders build leaders! However, leader development is highly complex and very little understood. This book examines core principles of leader development.

5. ***Leaders & Managers.*** Deals with the distinctions between leaders and managers. Contains extensive worksheets.

6. ***Abusive Leadership.*** A must read for all Christian leaders. Reveals the true natures and sources of abusive leadership and servant leadership.

7. ***Understanding Change.*** Leading change is one of the most difficult leadership responsibilities. It is also one of the most important. This book is an excellent primer that will help you understand resistance to change, the change process and how to help people through change.

8. ***Building Teams.*** What teams are and how they best work.

9. ***Understanding Organizations.*** A primer on organizational structure.

10. ***Women in Leadership.*** A biblical study concerning this very controversial issue.

11. ***Healthy Followers.*** The popular conception that "everything depends on leaders" is not entirely correct. Without thoughtful and active followers, the greatest of leaders will fail. This book studies the characteristics of healthy followers and is also a great resource for team building.

12. ***Listening.*** Listening is one of the most important of all leadership skills. This book studies how we can be better listeners and better leaders.

13. ***Transformational Thinking.*** This book introduces a new model of transformational thinking – of loving God with our minds – that identifies the critical thinking capacities of a healthy Christian leader. In addition, practical ways of nurturing those thinking capacities are described.

Strategic Press
www.StrategicPress.org

Strategic Press is a division of Strategic Global Assistance, Inc.
www.sgai.org

513 S. Main St. Suite 2
Elkhart, IN 46516
U.S.A

+1-844-532-3371 (LEADER-1)

www.ingramcontent.com/pod-product-compliance
Lightning Source LLC
LaVergne TN
LVHW051210080426
835512LV00019B/3188